ZEBRA MIGRATION

BY L. E. CARMICHAEL

The Child's World®

Published by The Child's World®
1980 Lookout Drive • Mankato, MN 56003-1705
800-599-READ • www.childsworld.com

ACKNOWLEDGMENTS
The Child's World®: Mary Berendes, Publishing Director
Content Consultant: Dr. Tanya Dewey,
   University of Michigan Museum of Zoology
The Design Lab: Design and production
Red Line Editorial: Editorial direction

PHOTO CREDITS
Michael Inselmann/Dreamstime, cover (top), 1, back cover; Johannes
Gerhardus Swanepoel/Dreamstime, cover (bottom), 2-3; Vibe Images/
Shutterstock Images, 4-5; XNR Productions, 7; Marina Cano/Dreamstime,
8; Mogens Trolle/iStockphoto, 10; Eric Isselée/Dreamstime, 11; Ralf
Herschbach/Shutterstock Images, 12-13; Jean-marc Strydom/Dreamstime,
14-15; East Village Images/Shutterstock Images, 16-17; Darko Komorski/
Dreamstime, 18; Nick Biemans/Bigstock, 20-21; Hongqi Zhang/Bigstock,
22; Oleg Znamenskiy/Dreamstime, 23; Daniel Boiteau/Dreamstime, 24;
Dirk/Dreamstime, 26-27; Shutterstock Images, 28-29

Design elements: Michael Inselmann/Dreamstime

ISBN 9781609736279
LCCN 2011940068

Printed in the United States of America

ABOUT THE AUTHOR: Lindsey E. Carmichael earned a PhD for studying the migration of wolves and arctic foxes in Canada's North. Now she writes nonfiction for children and contributes to the science blog, Sci/Why. There are no zebras in Nova Scotia, where Lindsey lives, but she'd love to see them in the wild someday.

TABLE OF CONTENTS

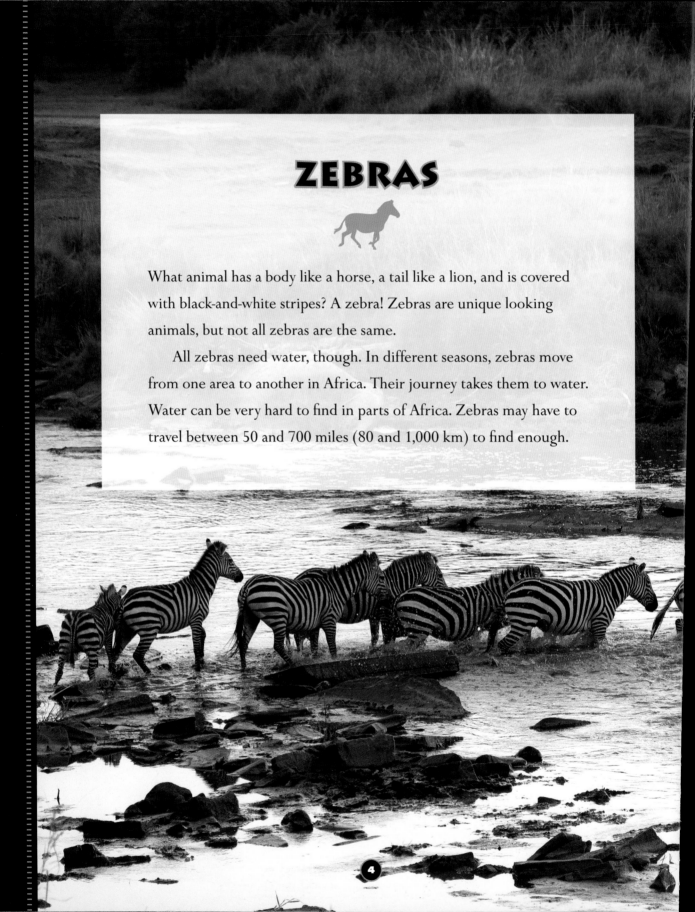

ZEBRAS

What animal has a body like a horse, a tail like a lion, and is covered with black-and-white stripes? A zebra! Zebras are unique looking animals, but not all zebras are the same.

All zebras need water, though. In different seasons, zebras move from one area to another in Africa. Their journey takes them to water. Water can be very hard to find in parts of Africa. Zebras may have to travel between 50 and 700 miles (80 and 1,000 km) to find enough.

The zebra's lifetime journey is its migration. This is when an animal moves from one **habitat** to another. Migrations happen for many reasons. Some animals move to be in warmer weather where there is more food. There they can reproduce, or have their babies. And these migrations can be short distances, such as from a mountaintop to its valley. Or they can be long distances, like the zebra's journey.

Zebras migrate to find water and food.

MIGRATION MAP

Different types of zebras migrate different ways. Some zebras move short distances over the land. They look for food but stay close to water. They do not follow a regular path. Other zebras follow trails up and down mountains. They go higher up or lower down depending on the season.

The biggest zebra migration happens in the Serengeti-Mara **Ecosystem** of Kenya and Tanzania. In September and October, zebras live in Kenya. This is the most northern place they visit. Around November, they start moving south into Tanzania. In March or April, the zebras change direction. They head northwest. In July or August, they turn northeast and end up back in Kenya. These zebras have a **seasonal** and **latitudinal** migration. In some years, their path looks a bit like a triangle. Other times, zebras travel in a line that goes north and south.

The map shows the migration of plains zebras in the Serengeti-Mara Ecosystem.

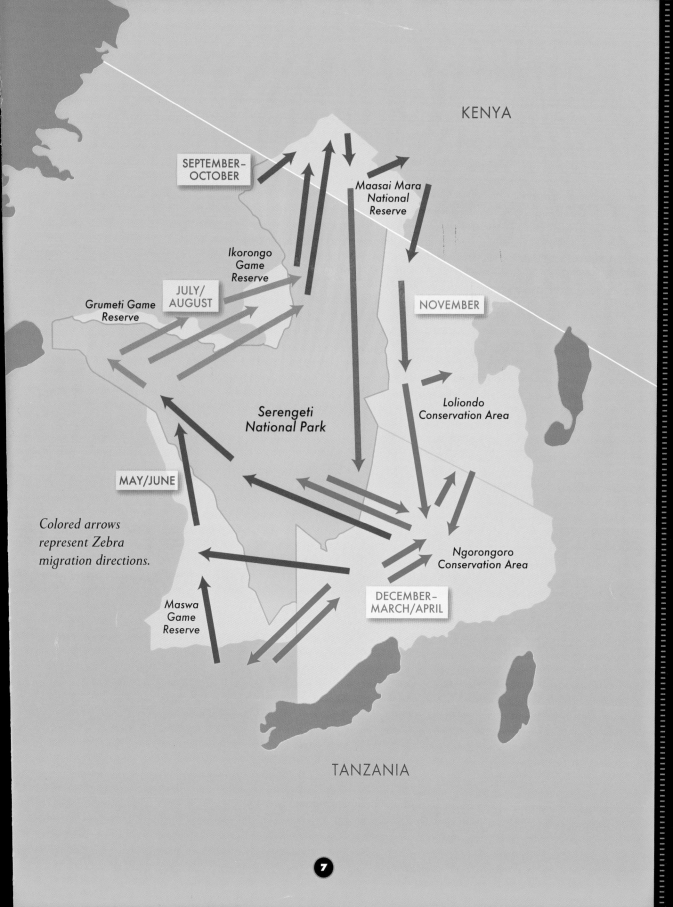

KENYA

SEPTEMBER–
OCTOBER

Maasai Mara
National
Reserve

Ikorongo
Game
Reserve

JULY/
AUGUST

NOVEMBER

Grumeti Game
Reserve

Serengeti
National Park

Loliondo
Conservation Area

MAY/JUNE

*Colored arrows
represent Zebra
migration directions.*

Ngorongoro
Conservation Area

Maswa
Game
Reserve

DECEMBER–
MARCH/APRIL

TANZANIA

*Grévy's zebras are the
largest type of zebra.*

TYPES OF ZEBRAS

There are three different types of zebras in Africa. Grévy's zebras are the largest of the three. They have large round ears like mules. Their stripes are narrow and their bellies are white. Grévy's zebras live in northern Kenya and southern Ethiopia. They prefer to live in grasslands. Their habitat is known as a **savanna**.

Grévy's zebras are not very social. If they come together in groups, the groups do not last long. Males are called stallions. Each stallion finds a piece of land for his territory. Stallions mark the edges of their territories with droppings. Other males smell the droppings and know not to enter. When it is time to mate, females visit the males with the best territories. The rest of the year, mothers live with their babies, called foals.

Mountain zebras are the smallest type. They live in two kinds of groups. A **harem** is made up of one stallion and up to six mares and their foals. Young males live with other **bachelors**. When males are old enough to mate, they find female zebras. These females form a new harem.

Mountain zebras are found in the mountains. They have sharp, narrow hooves. They help the zebras climb up and down rocky trails. Mountain zebras live in South Africa and Namibia.

The most common type of zebra is the plains zebra. These zebras are found in many countries across eastern and southern Africa. They live in different habitats, but are most often found in savannas. Trees are far apart in these areas. Plains zebras have stripes that run all the way under their bellies. They live in harems and bachelor groups. Sometimes, plains zebras will join together to form larger herds.

Female mountain zebras live in a harem.

ZEBRA STRIPES ARE LIKE A HUMAN'S FINGERPRINTS. NO TWO ZEBRAS HAVE THE SAME STRIPES.

WALKING TO WATER

Zebras rely on water, which can sometimes be hard to find in Africa. There is plenty of water during the wet season. This lasts from November to March. It rains hard and often during this time of year. Lakes and rivers overflow. Pure, fresh water collects in hollows on the ground. During the wet season, zebras have plenty to drink wherever they go.

The dry season is very different. The rains stop falling. As the months go by, the grass turns dry and brown. Zebras usually stay within 7 to 12 miles (12 to 20 km) of lakes and rivers during the dry season.

In the rainy season, water collects on the ground.

Female Grévy's zebras need water every other day when they have new foals. Without babies, Grévy's zebras can go up to five days without drinking. Even so, they live near fixed water sources, such as big rivers or lakes. When rivers run low, Grévy's zebras use their hooves. They dig until they find moisture. Zebras defend their water holes against other animals. The zebras attack or chase the animals away.

In the dry season, staying near water is important. But, it creates a new problem. Sometimes, so many animals gather around water that they eat all the food in the area. Zebras are **grazers**. They like to eat grass. When the grass is gone, zebras might eat leaves or roots. Often, it is better to move to a place where grass is still growing.

To nurse their young, Grévy's zebras need water every other day.

ZEBRAS CAN RUN
UP TO 40 MILES PER
HOUR (65 KMH).

DIFFERENT MIGRATIONS

Grévy's zebras do not normally migrate. They live by large bodies of water and usually have enough food to eat. But, sometimes there are **droughts**. In these years, the zebras travel as far as 50 miles (80 km) in search of water.

Migration is a normal part of a mountain zebra's life. During the wet season, mountain zebras live on low foothills and plains. They find plenty of grass to eat there. As the dry season begins, mountain zebras climb uphill to pools and springs. This is called **altitudinal** migration.

Of the three types, plains zebras need the most water. They can become weak if they do not drink every day. That makes it harder to outrun **predators** such as lions and hyenas. When the land is very dry, it is also hard to find enough food. Mothers might not be able to make milk for their young. Up to half of the zebra foals born in drought years die.

Like mountain zebras, plains zebras find water and food by migrating. Their route takes them north and south, and sometimes east and west.

Mountain zebras move up and down mountains when they migrate.

THE SERENGETI-MARA ECOSYSTEM

Serengeti National Park is in Tanzania. This country is on the eastern coast of Africa. The Maasai people call this area *Siringitu*. That means "the place where the land moves on forever." Kenya is just north of the Serengeti. It is where the Maasai Mara Wildlife **Reserve** is located. Together, they make up the Serengeti-Mara Ecosystem.

Many animals migrate in the Serengeti-Mara Ecosystem.

Grasslands stretch across the land. Where rivers cross the savanna, acacia, mahogany, and fig trees grow near them. The Serengeti-Mara covers 25,000 square miles (40,000 sq km). It is home to elephants, antelope, ostriches, hyenas, lions, cheetahs, and monkeys. But, this protected area exists to help the migrating animals. The ecosystem's borders were set to match the yearly path of these animals. Fossils show us that mammals have been migrating in the Serengeti-Mara Ecosystem for more than 1 million years. Scientists believe there are 660,000 plains zebras in Africa. Of those, 200,000 live in the Serengeti-Mara.

Zebras find shade from the hot sun.

THE GREAT MIGRATION

It is the dry season. The grasses are brown and the soil is cracked. Waves of heat rise from the earth. In the Mara area, the only growing things are found by lakes and rivers. That is where the zebras are, too.

The zebras sleep near the water. In the daytime, they make short trips in search of food. Last year's foals rest in the cool shade. They lay their heads on each other's shoulders.

It is November, and a cloud is forming in the southern sky. The harem becomes nervous. Zebras call to each other. They make a sound like "kwa-he!" It is time for the rains and the migration to begin.

Each harem of plains zebras has a **dominant** mare. The dominant mare is usually the oldest. When the migration begins, this dominant mare leads the way. The other mares and foals form a line behind her. The stallion walks in the rear. He watches for lions and other predators. When the harem meets other groups of zebras, the groups travel together as one large herd.

From the Mara region, the herds move south into the Serengeti. Zebras move toward the rain. A few days after a storm, grass grows. The savanna turns green. Zebras arrive just in time for a feast. After grazing, they drink from pools made by the rain.

By January, the herds reach the southern Serengeti. That is where this year's new foals are born. Stallions guard the mares while they give birth. Zebra foals can stand up when they are only 15 or 20 minutes old.

In a few hours, the foals are strong enough to follow the herd. Young zebras will stay near their mothers for up to three years. Each year, they take part in the migration. When they leave the harem, they will know where to migrate.

By the time May ends, the rains are almost gone. Small pools start to disappear. The hot sun beats down on the savanna. It is a sign that the dry season has begun. Plains zebras change direction now. They travel northwest across the Serengeti. When the grass dries out in June or July, the zebras turn north. By August, they arrive back at the Maasai Mara Wildlife Reserve. The zebra's journey can be as long as 700 miles (1,100 km). It takes nine months to complete.

Zebra foals can stand soon after they are born.

LAWNMOWERS OF THE SERENGETI

Scientists guess that 2 million animals migrate in the Serengeti-Mara. That includes wildebeests and Thompson's gazelles, too. Even though zebras are just a part of this group, they have a very important job to do.

Savanna grasses can grow very tall. The softest and healthiest grass is at the bottom of the stalk, near the ground. The old grass at the top of the stalk is tough. It has fewer **nutrients**. Wildebeests and gazelles cannot eat the old, tough grass, but zebras can.

Zebras' stomachs can get the nutrients from the grass quickly. They eat a lot of tough grass. This gives the zebras the same amount of nutrients they would from eating a small amount of good grass. That is why zebras graze for up to 18 hours every day. They crop the grass very short. That is why they are known as the lawnmowers of the Serengeti.

Zebras eat the long, tough parts of grass on the savanna.

Wildebeests follow zebras and eat the soft grasses left behind.

When the rains start and fresh grass shoots up, zebras are the first animals to arrive. They eat their fill and move on to a new patch. Wildebeests follow zebras. They eat the softer, shorter grass left behind.

The zebra's grazing habits are good for wildebeests. They are also good for zebras. Rain comes to the savanna around the same time every year. However, the rain never falls in exactly the same place. Because zebras can eat tougher food, they have more options when they pick their route. They can also take a different route in different years.

Wildebeests also benefit zebras. Lions will not hunt zebras if wildebeests are around. Wildebeests are smaller and easier for lions to catch. So, zebras are less likely to be eaten.

Poachers kill zebras for their skins.

ONE ZEBRA SKIN CAN BE WORTH UP TO $2,000 TO POACHERS.

THREATS TO ZEBRAS

Zebras have been hunted for their skins. The hide of the quagga, a type of plains zebra, was once popular. Between 1700 and 1900, many quaggas were killed. Today, they are **extinct**.

In the 1930s, Cape mountain zebras nearly went extinct, too. But, people created parks to protect them. Fifteen hundred Cape mountain zebras are alive today. Scientists believe more than 25,000 Hartmann's mountain zebras also survive. Between 2,000 and 3,000 Hartmann's zebras are legally killed every year.

Poachers are a bigger threat to mountain zebras. Poachers are people who hunt wildlife illegally. They use zebra meat for food. They also make money selling zebra skins. The skins are made into rugs, coats, or purses.

Poachers also kill Grévy's zebras, because of the narrow stripes of their coats. Forty years ago, 15,000 Grévy's zebras lived over northeastern Africa. Now, they are found only in Kenya and southern Ethiopia. Only 2,500 are left. Grévy's zebras are **endangered** animals. Like the quagga, they could disappear forever.

Another threat to zebras is farming. Where humans are not growing plant crops, they raise cows, horses, or pigs. These farms are big threats to zebras.

Most Grévy's zebras live in areas where there is farming. Farmers use water that zebras need on farm fields. Cows drink from the zebra's water holes and graze the same fields.

Scientists have shown that Grévy's zebras like to live in areas where there are no cows. They do not have to share water. Sometimes Grévy's zebras cannot find land without cows. Then they have to migrate farther from water to get enough food. Farming is a threat to plains zebras and Hartmann's mountain zebras, too.

But, some people are trying to help zebras. In Namibia, people have made water holes for Hartmann's zebras to use. This allows zebras to live in areas where they normally could not survive. It also causes zebras to move away from farm areas.

The large space that zebras need to live can put them at risk. Zebras need habitat for both the wet season and the dry season. They also need migration paths. These paths allow zebras to travel from one habitat to another. If these paths are destroyed, zebras may not find their way to water.

People are helping Hartmann's zebras find water.

HELP FOR ZEBRAS

Governments in Africa are creating parks to help zebras. These parks give zebras a place to live. Sometimes parks have fences and guards to help keep poachers out. More water holes are being dug so zebras and cows do not have to share. Local people help scientists find out what zebras need to survive. They also check to see if zebra **populations** are getting smaller.

Reserves have been made for migrating zebras.

When populations shrink, it can be easier for every animal to find food and water. That may mean that zebras will not have a reason to migrate. Some small groups of plains zebras have stopped migrating. They stay near their water holes all year round.

Even if zebras still live in Africa, their migration may not continue. Scientists, governments, farmers, and hunters in Africa are trying to stop this from happening. By working together, they hope to keep the zebras moving for years to come.

TYPES OF MIGRATION

Different animals migrate for different reasons. Some move because of the climate. Some travel to find food or a mate. Here are the different types of animal migration:

Seasonal migration: This type of migration happens when the seasons change. Most animals migrate for this reason. Other types of migration, such as altitudinal and latitudinal, may also include seasonal migration.

Latitudinal migration: When animals travel north and south, it is called latitudinal migration. Doing so allows animals to change the climate where they live.

Altitudinal migration: This migration happens when animals move up and down mountains. In summer, animals can live higher on a mountain. During the cold winter, they move down to lower and warmer spots.

Reproductive migration: Sometimes animals move to have their babies. This migration may keep the babies safer when they are born. Or babies may need a certain habitat to live in after birth.

Nomadic migration: Animals may wander from place to place to find food in this type of migration.

Complete migration: This type of migration happens when animals are finished mating in an area. Then almost all of the animals leave the area. They may travel more than 15,000 miles (25,000 km) to spend winters in a warmer area.

Partial migration: When some, but not all, animals of one type move away from their mating area, it is partial migration. This is the most common type of migration.

Irruptive migration: This type of migration may happen one year, but not the next. It may include some or all of a type of animal. And the animal group may travel short or long distances.

> SOMETIMES ANIMALS NEVER COME BACK TO A PLACE WHERE THEY ONCE LIVED. THIS CAN HAPPEN WHEN HUMANS OR NATURE DESTROY THEIR HABITAT. FOOD, WATER, OR SHELTER MAY BECOME HARD TO FIND. OR A GROUP OF ANIMALS MAY BECOME TOO LARGE FOR AN AREA. THEN THEY MUST MOVE TO FIND FOOD.

GLOSSARY

altitudinal (AL-ti-tude-uh-nal): Altitudinal is something that is done from different heights above the ground. Mountain zebras have an altitudinal migration.

bachelors (BACH-uh-lurz): Bachelors are single males. Zebras live in harems or groups of bachelors.

dominant (DOM-uh-nuhnt): A dominant animal has the most power in a group. The oldest female is dominant.

droughts (DROUTZ): Droughts are long times of dry weather. Droughts make the water in an area dry up.

ecosystem (EE-koh-siss-tuhm): An ecosystem is a community of plants and animals that depend on each other and the land. Each animal and plant is needed to balance an ecosystem.

endangered (en-DAYN-jurd): An animal is endangered when it is at risk of disappearing forever. Grévy's zebras are endangered animals.

extinct (ek-STINGKT): A type of animal is extinct if it has died out. The quagga became extinct.

grazers (GRAYZ-urz): Grazers are animals that eat grass for food. Zebras are grazers.

habitat (HAB-uh-tat): A habitat is a place that has the food, water, and shelter an animal needs to survive. Zebras move from one habitat to another when they migrate.

harem (HAIR-uhm): A harem is a group of female animals that share one mate. A harem may have a dominant female.

latitudinal (LAT-uh-tood-i-nul): Latitudinal relates to how far north and south something is from the equator. Plains zebras have a latitudinal migration path.

nutrients (NOO-tree-untz): Nutrients are things that people, animals, and plants need to stay alive. Tough grasses have the nutrients zebras need.

populations (pop-yuh-LAY-shuhnz): Populations are the animals of one type that live in the same area. Some populations of zebras are shrinking.

predators (PRED-uh-turs): Predators are animals that hunt and eat other animals. Lions are predators of zebras.

reserve (ri-ZURV): A reserve is a place that is set aside to keep animals and plants safe. Many zebras live and migrate on a reserve.

savanna (suh-VAN-uh): A savanna is a flat, grassy area with few or no trees. Plains zebras live on the savanna.

seasonal (SEE-zuhn-uhl): Seasonal is something related to the seasons of the year. Plains zebras have a seasonal migration.

FURTHER INFORMATION

Books

Carney, Elizabeth. *Great Migrations: Whales, Wildebeests, Butterflies, Elephants, and Other Amazing Animals on the Move.* Washington, D.C.: National Geographic, 2010.

Giles, Bridget. *Animal Families: Zebras.* Danbury, CT: Grolier Educational, 2001

Noble-Goodman, Katherine. *Animals, Animals: Zebras.* New York: Marshall Cavendish, 2006.

Web Sites

Visit our Web site for links about zebra migration: *childsworld.com/links*

Note to Parents, Teachers, and Librarians: We routinely verify our Web links to make sure they are safe and active sites. So encourage your readers to check them out!

INDEX